Non-Fiction
Teaching Notes

Manda George

Contents

	Introduction	3
	How to introduce the books	3
	Cross-curricular links with QCA/NLS objectives	4
	Levels chart	5
Hard Work	Reading the book with individuals or guided reading groups	6
	Further reading activities	7
	Speaking and listening activities	8
	ICT links	8
	Writing	8
Making Music	Reading the book with individuals or guided reading groups	9
	Further reading activities	10
	Speaking and listening activities	11
	ICT links	11
	Writing	11
Save our Coasts!	Reading the book with individuals or guided reading groups	12
	Further reading activities	13
	Speaking and listening activities	14
	ICT links	14
	Writing	14
Under the Volcano	Reading the book with individuals or guided reading groups	15
	Further reading activities	16
	Speaking and listening activities	17
	ICT links	17
	Writing	17
Winning Words	Reading the book with individuals or guided reading groups	18
	Further reading activities	19
	Speaking and listening activities	19
	ICT links	19
	Writing	20
Wonderful Things	Reading the book with individuals or guided reading groups	21
	Further reading activities	22
	Speaking and listening activities	22
	ICT links	23
	Writing	23
	Links to other *TreeTops* and OUP titles	24

Introduction

TreeTops Non-Fiction is an exciting extension to the *TreeTops* range. All the titles have been chosen to appeal to 7–11 year olds and have an appropriate reading ability level at their particular Stage. *TreeTops* Stages follow on from the *Oxford Reading Tree* Stages, and are designed to be used flexibly with your individual pupil's reading ability. The levelling guide on page 5 gives you an indication of how the Stages correspond to the Year and age of the average pupil, together with the relevant match from the National Curriculum Level or Scottish, Northern Irish and Welsh equivalents.

Each book includes a Contents page, an Index and/or a Glossary of specialist terms or equivalent. These features enable teachers to develop children's information retrieval skills. In addition, features of non-fiction texts, such as sub-headings, text boxes and captions help children learn to skim read a text for information. The series aims to fascinate children with surprising and interesting information.

How to introduce the books

Before reading the book, always read the title and talk about the possible content. Encourage the children to articulate what they already know about the subject, what they would like to find out and how they will use this book to do it. Complete the reading session with the pupils telling you what they have learned.

This booklet provides suggestions for using this book with groups of pupils or individuals. Suggestions are also provided for speaking and listening, further reading activities, ICT links and writing. These may be used as a follow-on to the reading or used at another time.

Guided Reading Cards with built-in comprehension are available for each book. These provide detailed guidance for using the book for guided reading. Parental notes are included in each individual book.

Cross-curricular links with QCA/NLS objectives

Title	QCA Cross-curricular links	NLS objectives
Hard Work	History 11 What was it like for children living in Victorian Britain?	Y5T1 T21 to identify the features of recounted texts Y5T1 T24 to write recounts based on subject, topic
Making Music	Design & Technology 5a Musical instruments Music 21 Who knows? – Exploring musical processes	Y5T1 T21 to identify the features of recounted texts Y5T1 T24 to write recounts based on personal experience
Save our Coasts!	Geography 23 Investigating coasts	Y5T2 T17 to locate information confidently and efficiently through i) using contents, indexes, sections, headings, ii) skimming to gain overall sense of text, iii) scanning to locate specific information, iv) close reading to aid understanding
Under the Volcano	Geography 24 Passport to the world	Y5T1 T21 to identify the features of recounted texts, including introduction to orientate reader; chronological sequence; supporting illustrations
Winning Words	English 9b print and ICT based reference and information materials	Y5T2 T17 to locate information confidently and efficiently through i) using contents, indexes, sections, headings, ii) skimming to gain overall sense of text, iii) scanning to locate specific information, iv) close reading to aid understanding, v) using CD ROM and other IT sources, where available
Wonderful Things	Art & Design 5b Containers 5c Talking textiles	Y5T1 T26 to make notes for different purposes, e.g. noting key points as a record of what has been read

Levels chart

Title	Treetops Tops Stage 13	England NC level	Scotland	N Ireland	Wales
Hard Work	Year 5 Terms 1 and 2 Ages 9–10	Level 3/4	Level C/D	**Reading Activities:** a b f h i Outcomes: a b e g h k **Writing** Opportunities: b c d e Outcomes: b c e f g h	**Reading:** Range: 1 2 3 4 5 Skills: 1 2 3 5 6 7 8 9 Language development: 1 2 **Writing:** Range: 1 4 5 Skills: 1 2 3 5 6 Language development: 1 2 5 6
Making Music	Year 5 Terms 1 and 2 Ages 9–10	Level 3/4	Level C/D		
Save our Coasts!	Year 5 Terms 1 and 2 Ages 9–10	Level 3/4	Level C/D		
Under the Volcano	Year 5 Terms 1 and 2 Ages 9–10	Level 3/4	Level C/D		
Winning Words	Year 5 Terms 1 and 2 Ages 9–10	Level 3/4	Level C/D		
Wonderful Things	Year 5 Terms 1 and 2 Ages 9–10	Level 3/4	Level C/D		

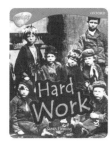

Hard Work

Reading the book with individuals or guided reading groups

Introducing the book
- Look together at the cover and read the title. Ask the children to look for clues on the cover to suggest whether the book is fiction or non-fiction.
- Read the Contents page together and ask the children to discuss previous knowledge about working children in the past.
- Read pages 4 and 5 together and ask the children to answer the questions and discuss any work that they have to do, either at home or at school.
- Explain to children that the book contains eyewitness accounts and ask them to consider how this helps the reader.

Strategy check
- Remind the children about the strategies they can use to work out new words, e.g. breaking down words, such as 'compulsory', into syllables.
- Model for children how to reread a sentence to work out the meanings of unfamiliar words and phrases.

Focus of reading
- Explain that while reading the text, you want the children to think about how it felt to be a working child in the past.
- Encourage them to look closely at the eyewitness accounts to find evidence to support their ideas.

Independent reading
- Observe the strategies the children use to work out new words, and offer support as appropriate. Encourage the children to refer to the Glossary definitions at the back of the book, if they do not understand the meaning of an emboldened word.
- Praise children who reread sentences to check for meaning.

Return and respond to the text
- Come together and ask the children to describe how it felt to be a working child in the past. Encourage them to use evidence from the text to support their ideas.
- Look together at the eyewitness account in quotation marks on page 15. Ask the children to consider the purpose of this part of the text and how it helps the reader. Why do they think the author has decided to include these personal anecdotes?
- Discuss how and why the laws changed about children at work. Ask the children to find the information about the laws that were introduced to help working children. Do they think they actually helped? Why or why not?
- Ask the children to consider which job they would have undertaken and why. Did some jobs seem harder work than others?

Further reading activities
- Ask the children to scan the text and create a list of the jobs mentioned. Ask them to match eyewitness accounts with the jobs on the list. With a partner, they could then go on to discuss and rank the jobs in order of hardship.
- The child might like to read *Victorian Children* from Oxford Connections to find out more about children living in Victorian times. Are there any similarities or differences between the two books?

Speaking and listening activities
- With the children, look at the list of jobs undertaken by Janet Bathgate on page 13. Use 'hot seating' techniques to encourage the children to consider how Janet felt when she was working.
- Use a drama session to explore some of the different jobs mentioned in the text.

ICT links
- Using the Internet, ask the children to view Victorian history websites to find further eyewitness accounts from working children in the past, and evaluate the way the information is presented. Encourage them to be critical of the modes of presentation. Were any sites more successful than others in doing this?

Writing
- Explain to children that they are going to write a diary entry written from the point of view of Janet Bathgate. Discuss how the writing will be in the first person and the past tense.
- Model the diary opening for the children.
- Encourage the children to write about how Janet felt as she was working.

Making Music

Reading the book with individuals or guided reading groups

Introducing the book

- Look together at the cover of the book and read the title. Ask the children to suggest what sort of book this is, i.e. fiction or non-fiction.
- Ask the children to suggest what they might find out by reading this book.
- Look at the Contents page and ask the children to consider whether they think the book should be read in sequence or can be dipped into.
- Revise some of the non-fiction features of information books and flick through the pages and ask the children, in turn, to find an example of each, e.g. recount (pages 10 and 11); explanation (page 6); instructional (page 13); report (page 22).
- Ask them to explain how the pictures and diagrams help the reader to understand the information.

Strategy check

- Remind the children about strategies they can use when they are unsure of the sense of a sentence, e.g. rereading the sentence, or covering up clauses within a long sentence to gain the general meaning, before going back to read the additional clauses, e.g. 'the pitch of the note – whether it is high or low – depends on the length of the tube.'
- Review some of the strategies the children can use when they meet a new or unfamiliar word.

Focus of reading
- Ask the children to look at the layout of the text in detail and to consider the different purpose of different sections of the text.
- Explain that they will be using some of the features of the structure and layout in their own writing later on.

Independent reading
- Observe the strategies used by the children to support their comprehension. Provide prompts and support if needed.
- Praise children for rereading text to check for meaning.
- Ask them to consider the purpose of different sections of the text.

Return and respond to the text
- Come together and discuss the different organisational features of the text. Ask the children to explain in their own words why they think the text has been organised in a particular way.
- Discuss the purpose of the *'Did you know?'* and *'Simon Says' boxes*. Ask the children to consider what they add to the text.
- Encourage the children to share one fact that they found funny or interesting.

Further reading activities
- Return to the Contents page and ask the children to select a topic that they would like to find out about.
- Ask them to choose a heading from the list and reread the section.
- Ask the children to explain to a partner what they found out in their own words, and encourage them to use the Glossary to support their understanding of new words.

Speaking and listening activities
- Listen to a selection of music from films. Ask the children to describe to a partner how the music makes them feel and to explore why.
- Use dance or drama sessions to develop children's ability to use their bodies in response to music.
- Ask children to evaluate their dance or drama performances.

ICT links
- Use a tape recorder to record sound effects around the school. Encourage children to use the tape recording to create a game for younger children. Can they guess which object is making the sound they can hear?
- Explore children's own musical compositions using the 'Making tracks' website: http://www.bbc.co.uk/radio3/makingtracks/

Writing
- Return to pages 10 and 11. Ask the children to reread Simon's account of his audition and to think about their own experiences of auditions or sports trials.
- Explain to children that you want them to write their own account of what happened and how they felt.
- Discuss with children how Simon organised his writing into paragraphs and support children to plan their writing carefully.
- When the writing is complete, ask the children to share their accounts with the rest of the group.

Save our Coasts!

Reading the book with individuals or guided reading groups

Introducing the book
- Look together at the front cover and read the title. Ask the children to consider whether this is a fiction or non-fiction book. How can they tell?
- Ask the children to suggest what they think the book will be about.
- Read the Contents page together and ask the children to read the introduction on pages 4 and 5. Establish how the book will focus on humans' impact on coastlines around the world.
- Flick through the pages together and discuss some of the features of the layout, and how they help the reader to understand the concepts explained in the text, e.g. 'The science: …' boxes on pages 12 and 16. How do the pictures and diagrams support the reader?
- Discuss whether the text needs to be read in sequence or whether the children can dip into specific sections.

Strategy check
- Remind the children about strategies they can use when they meet new words.
- Discuss with them the purpose of the Glossary and model how to use the Glossary effectively, using one of the emboldened words in the book.

Focus of reading
- Explain to the children that you want them to look closely at pages 12 to 21 and to consider some of the similarities and differences between the different areas of the world.
- Ask the children to make a note of three facts for each area.

Independent reading
- Observe the strategies used by children when they face new words, and prompt them as needed, e.g. splitting up compound words, such as 'longshore', to identify how it is read and to guess its meaning.
- Praise children who use the Glossary to support their understanding of new vocabulary.

Return and respond to the text
- Come together and ask the children to share the three facts about the coasts of the different areas of the world they noted down as part of their focus of reading.
- Ask the rest of the group to consider whether the facts have covered the most important information.
- Encourage the children to discuss the similarities and differences between the different coastlines.
- Discuss how the layout of the text on pages 12 to 21 supported them as they were trying to find out information. Were any sections more useful than others?
- Ask the children to share one new fact they found out during the course of their reading.

Further reading activities
- Ask the children to finish reading the text and note the key factors affecting the coastlines.
- Use a range of non-fiction texts and atlases to find additional information about the geographical areas. Support the children in keeping short notes from their reading.

Speaking and listening activities

- Divide the children into small groups and explain that they will be developing a presentation about coastlines for the rest of the class. You may like to allocate a particular geographical area to each group.
- Support the children in creating a short presentation in the role of environmental officers. Encourage them to use factual evidence to back up points they make during their presentation.

ICT links

- Children, in pairs, could create a short PowerPoint presentation about coastlines to show the rest of the class. Establish some design rules for developing their pages, e.g. consistent position and colour of buttons and icons, clarity of text and pictures.

Writing

- Using their notes gathered from reading, ask the children to create a simple table indicating the similarities and differences between the geographical areas in the text.
- Together create a writing frame to support the clear presentation of the information. Ask the children to consider appropriate headings for each section of the table.
- The completed tables of information could be used to form part of a classroom display.

Under the Volcano

Reading the book with individuals or guided reading groups

Introducing the book
- Look together at the front cover and ask the children to suggest whether the book will be fiction or non-fiction. Discuss the text types featured in the book, and ask the children to find an example of each, e.g. report (page 6); recount (pages 10 and 11); explanation (page 14).
- Ask the children to share any prior knowledge they have about volcanoes with a partner.
- Look together at the Contents page and remind the children of its purpose.
- Read the introduction together on page 4 and 5. What techniques has the author used to make the reader want to read on?
- Look together at pages 8 and 9. Ask the children to scan the text and discuss any unfamiliar vocabulary. Remind them about using the Glossary to help them with new words.

Strategy check
- Remind the children about the strategies they can use to work out new words, e.g. breaking down words, such as 'Herculaneum', into syllables.
- Revise what the children can do if they are unsure of the sense of a sentence, e.g. rereading the previous sentence and the one after it to help them guess the meaning of it.

Focus of reading
- Explain to the children that you will be asking them to summarise what they read about Pompeii and the eruption of Vesuvius, focusing on the salient points.
- Ask the children to read pages 6 to 13.

Independent reading
- Observe the strategies the children are using to help them with new words and provide support as needed.
- Praise children who refer to the Glossary for the meanings of new vocabulary.

Return and respond to the text
- Ask the children to share with a partner their summary of important events from their reading.
- Look together at the Key features box on page 11 and discuss how the information about volcanic eruptions has been summarised into short bullet points.
- Explore with the children any additional new words they read, and discuss the strategies they used to work them out.
- Discuss the eyewitness account on pages 10 and 11 and ask the children to consider why this has been included and what impact it has on the reader.

Further reading activities
- Ask the children to read pages 14 and 15 and to summarise the most important information, in bullet point form.
- Challenge the children to create a simple flow chart and label it to show how a volcano is formed and erupts.

Speaking and listening activities
- Choose one child to take on the role of Pliny and support the rest of the group in asking questions to find out what it was like on the day of the eruption.
- Use drama sessions to recreate the volcanic eruption and Pompeii being buried.

ICT links
- Encourage the children to view this website and evaluate its features in presenting information about volcanoes: http://www.nationalgeographic.com/ngkids/0312/main.html Can they think of other features that could have been used to enhance the presentation?

Writing
- Look at the visual timeline on pages 22 and 23. Discuss with the children the benefits of including such diagrams in non-fiction texts.
- Ask them to identify other sections of the text where the inclusion of a diagram or timeline would support the reader.
- Model for children how to make notes to summarise key bits of information.
- Support the children in organising their notes into chronological order.
- Help them to create a flowchart or timeline to summarise information for the reader.
- When the writing is completed, ask the children to consider whether the visual timeline is easier or more difficult to read.

Winning Words

Reading the book with individuals or guided reading groups

Introducing the book
- Look together at the front cover and discuss the title. Ask the children to consider what they think the book is going to be about. After quickly skimming through the book, ask the children to predict why the author might have used the word 'Winning' in the title.
- Read the Contents page together. Think about the use of questions as headings. What purpose do they serve?
- Discuss with the children how the text on each page provides an answer to the question used as a heading. Ask them to discuss how they think the writing will need to be organised in order to help the reader.
- Flick through the pages of the book and ask the children to share some of the organisational features they find.

Strategy check
- Remind the children of some of the strategies they can use to work out new words. Revise with children how to find a root word as a clue to the meaning of unfamiliar vocabulary, e.g. 'technological'.
- Ask the children if they feel they need to read the text in sequence or whether they can just dip into it to find specific information.

Focus of reading
- Explain to the children that you want them to find out some information about how dictionaries are compiled.
- Use the Contents page to find the relevant section and ask the children to focus their reading on pages 16 to 23.

Independent reading
- Observe the strategies the children use when they meet new vocabulary, and provide prompts and support as needed.
- While children are reading, encourage them to use morphology – word structure – to help their understanding of new words.

Return and respond to the text
- Come together and ask the children to explain in their own words how dictionaries are created, how they work and why we need them.
- Ask them to consider whether the questions used as headings were answered in the body of the text. Encourage them to use examples from the text to support their thinking.
- Ask the children to share one new piece of information they found out about dictionaries. Was there anything about compiling dictionaries that surprised them?

Further reading activities
- Ask the children to scan parts of the text to find some of the suggested activities they can do on their own. Allow them time to try out some of them, e.g. combining existing words to create new ones, suggesting word origins.

Speaking and listening activities
- Watch part of a *Countdown* episode together.
- Reread pages 6 and 7 before allowing children time to develop and play their own *Countdown* game, using suggestions from the text to support them.

ICT links
- Ask the children to find specific information in a CD ROM dictionary or encyclopedia. Support them in using their knowledge of alphabetical order and other organisational features to find information quickly and efficiently.

Writing

- Return to page 23 and look at the list of typical dictionary features.
- Look together at a range of dictionaries and find examples of headwords, usage notes, pronunciation help, etc.
- Explain to the children that they will be creating a class dictionary and will need to use some of the features in their own time.
- Provide them with a list of words linked to a curriculum area, e.g. Science. Ask the children to write simple definitions for the words.
- Once the definitions have been written, ask the children to work in groups to decide on the layout and structure of the dictionary.

Wonderful Things

Reading the book with individuals or guided reading groups

Introducing the book
- Look together at the cover. Discuss the title and ask children what they think the book will be about.
- Ask the children to discuss what sort of book this is and to scan the pages to find out what is the main text type used in the book, e.g. report. Notice how the text is made up of both chronological and non-chronological sections.
- Remind the children about the function and use of the Contents page. Model for children how to use the Contents page to find specific information.
- Ask them to flick through the pages and comment on the layout and organisation of the information. Why do they think most of the book comprises illustrations and photographs?

Strategy check
- Remind the children about the strategies they can use to find specific information in non-fiction texts.
- Ask them to review the strategies they can use to work out unfamiliar words.
- Model for children how to scan part of the text in order to find specific words or phrases.

Focus of reading
- Ask the children to focus on pages 18 and 19 during their reading and explain that they are going to summarise the information about the use of colour in objects later in the session.

Independent reading
- Observe the strategies the children use as they are reading and prompt them as appropriate.
- As children are reading, ask a key question and support them in scanning the text to find the specific information.
- Praise children who are self-correcting as they read.

Return and response to the text
- Come together and ask the children to share one thing they found out about the use of colour in objects during their reading. Encourage them to give an example from the text as evidence.
- Discuss how the layout of the text supports the reader. Ask how headings and sub-headings help to signal what the text is about and how the pictures support comprehension. Discuss how the design of the page is influenced by the content.
- Why is it important in a text like this to use clear paragraphing?

Further reading activities
- Ask the children to reread pages 18 and 19. Ask them to scan the text for key words and to note down the most important information. Can they summarise the information in no more than three sentences?

Speaking and listening activities
- Look together at pages 14 and 15. Discuss the notion of using objects to support storytelling.
- Provide the children with a picture or historical artefact and challenge them to create a story around the object.
- Once ideas for the story have been discussed, create a group story, with each child in the group providing one or two sentences, before passing the object on to the next child.

ICT links

- Look at the range of transforming techniques listed on page 23. Ask the children to select one of the techniques and to use the Internet to find out more information about it. They could use ICT to present the information as a quiz for other members of the class.

Writing

- Use the pictures on pages 30 and 31 as stimulus. Ask the children to match the captions to the pictures.
- Then ask them to add to the captions to create a fuller double page spread.
- Encourage the children to use some of the organisation techniques seen in the book (headings, sub-headings, bullet points, etc.).

Links to other TreeTops and OUP titles

Oxford Literacy Web Non-Fiction KS2
True stories Stage 10
TreeTops True Stories Stages 13–14

TreeTops non-fiction Stage 13	*TreeTops* and OUP titles with similar subjects/themes
Hard Work	Oxford Connections *Victorian Children*
Making Music	Oxford Literacy Web *Music Makers* Oxford Web Spiders *What's it Like to Play in a Band?*
Save our Coasts!	Oxford Connections *Water and Rivers* Oxford Connections *Improving the Environment*
Under the Volcano	Oxford Connections *Mountains*
Winning Words	Oxford Concise School Dictionary Oxford Concise School Thesaurus Oxford Concise School Dictionary of Word Origins Oxford Literacy Web *The Invention of Games*
Wonderful Things	

OXFORD
UNIVERSITY PRESS

Great Clarendon Street, Oxford OX2 6DP

Oxford University Press is a department of the University of Oxford. It furthers the University's objective of excellence in research, scholarship, and education by publishing worldwide in

Oxford New York

Auckland Cape Town Dar es Salaam Hong Kong Karachi
Kuala Lumpur Madrid Melbourne Mexico City Nairobi
New Delhi Shanghai Taipei Toronto

With offices in

Argentina Austria Brazil Chile Czech Republic France Greece
Guatemala Hungary Italy Japan Poland Portugal Singapore
South Korea Switzerland Thailand Turkey Ukraine Vietnam
Oxford is a registered trade mark of Oxford University Press in the UK and in certain other countries

© Oxford University Press 2005

The moral rights of the author have been asserted

Database right Oxford University Press (maker)

First published 2005

All rights reserved. No part of this publication may be reproduced, stored in a retrieval system, or transmitted, in any form or by any means, without the prior permission in writing of Oxford University Press, or as expressly permitted by law, or under terms agreed with the appropriate reprographics rights organization. Enquiries concerning reproduction outside the scope of the above should be sent to the Rights Department, Oxford University Press, at the address above

You must not circulate this book in any other binding or cover and you must impose this same condition on any acquirer

British Library Cataloguing in Publication Data

Data available

ISBN 978-0-19-919877-1

10 9 8 7 6

Page make-up by Fakenham Photosetting Ltd, Fakenham, Norfolk

Printed in China by Imago